FEEL YOUR LIFE

POOJA SINGH

ISBN 979-888530932-5

Contents

Acknowledgements *v*

About The Author *vii*

1. The Father 1
2. Train Your Mind For A Happy Life 3
3. A Decision Taking Process 4
4. Having A Aim Is Necessary 6
5. Keep Going On 7
6. Menstruation 8
7. Quotes By Pooja Singh 10
8. When You Are In Approach – Avoidance 29
9. Consternation... 30
10. Make Your Wishes.. 31
11. Love And Hate 32
12. Let Me Line 33
13. Let Your Feelings Out 34

Acknowledgements

This is my first solo book... Previously I have worked in three anthologies. I am a upsc aspirant and this journey of preparation has been widening my knowledge area continuously... My life ethic rules are inspired by it. There are very few people in my life who are close to me. I am blessed with the beautiful family.. My inspiration...and my support system. My father who always sees me like a achiever and encourage me to keep moving in my way. My mother... She never let me fall .. always help me to get over from my failure.. She is truly a inspiration for me. My elder brother Ashish Kumar Singh always teachs me the best lessons of my life and encourage me to follow my passion... That's why I am here. My younger sister Rashmi Singh and brother Shubham Singh... They both don't let me lose my hope. My Best friend Pooja Yadav... She is truly a blessing... A support system and a knowledge giver in my life. A very special thanks to my fiance "Shiv" to be in my life... You teach me to face the life in its real terms without any hesitation... With you this life will be a beautiful journey. And last but not the least... Mr. Shailesh Soni... big brother in my life... You have taught me the life. One more special person I really want to mention my multi talented Poonam di to encourage me to write more better.

About The Author

Pooja Singh

I have been a passionate writer and keen observer.. use to empathize with the situations and conditions of people to know what their feelings and emotions are...lead me to write this book. I am enjoying the phase, going through.. just want to tell the readers of this book.. go with the flow when you can't figure out what is happening in your life.. seriously life is too short for always making complains and for your infinite unlisted wishes too... every moment gonna leave you with some clues to step ahead and explore yourself. You only need to allow positive vibes to reach you and whenever you struggle with negativity, think opposite of that thought as everyone knows negative - negative end up with positive.. so train your mind, channelize your energy and start working on your wishes. Instead of looking for an ANGEL send by the GOD.. just be your own Angel by keeping yourself happy, confident and hopeful for every upcoming moments. YOUR LIFE IS YOUR KINGDOM AND YOU ARE THE KING.

My email - arju1234ppp@gmail.com

for any enquiry.

ONE

THE FATHER

A Mother is aware of your little things from the very first day you come into existence.. but the Father is the person who makes every effort to give a comfortable life to his children from the day you come into this world from the womb of mother.. he doesn't even know how to take you in his lap... Still, he brings everything to keep you happy... even do overtime to fulfill your desires. He used to look for a discount when tries to get something for himself but buys the best for his children.. even when the thing is costly enough to go out of budget. He never expresses his love.. but his actions do.

His one-time anger works as a dose for months.. and the love he shows after beating you... totally unparalleled. You may have explored the world but He knows the world. "Father, a family's backbone, a daughter's first love, and an ideal for a son.

There is a communication gap between a child and a father and that makes it a generation gap because of less interaction. A child goes to his father for permission, pocket money, and for the work which needs him. He wants to spend time with you but don't know how... he wants to talk to you but don't know how to start. He understands you and your feelings... your needs but doesn't know how to make you understand that he is concerned for you.

That's the story of almost every father but he can't express how much he loves you. Here you can start... have some evening tea with him or spent some time with him whenever he available share with him some experience and events of your life.. ask him "Papa.!!! how was your childhood..." it will take time but when the conversation starts and both of you open up... hours will fly away and you don't even realize about it.

TWO

TRAIN YOUR MIND FOR A HAPPY LIFE

You have to train your mind to keep yourself happy... Everything takes time sometimes more than your patience when failures wondering around you. It is your target, your responsibility to create ways for it to reach its destination and a happy and irrelevant stuff-free mind helps you to be there.. life always try to manipulate you to survive in the easiest way one can but it depends on you how you want to survive.. how you want to live your single moment of life... We are humans , a continuous evolving species with our innovative mind set to be superior , can do anything what we want. Action, Experience & Learning are the things which make you feel alive. Ya.. everyone makes mistakes but the best thing is when you choose the experience and your evolved maturity after that action that's what make you better.

THREE

A DECISION TAKING PROCESS

Yesss... It totally depends on the person who takes a decision. First thing, if you have been given the freedom to choose the path of your life, you are blessed.. second thing, just prove those persons right who give you that freedom. Every Decision leads you somewhere it may be drag you into the worst situation, a dark sight, but teaches you one of the best lessons of life, steps you take to overcome from that situation make you a grown-up person enough to not repeat that thought process again. It also happens that we make decisions but not work on the process the way we thought of doing that action, this may also lead to bad outcomes. So, what should be done to make the right decisions in life even in the worst demanding situation, STEPS can be followed:-

- First, choose the place where you feel calm and sit silently, let your mind relax from every kind of thought. It may take time but do it until you feel relaxed.

- Now when you are in relaxed mode, take a page and write down in sections.. what outcome you want from your action.. have you ever been in that situation, if there is anyone close with whom you can share it... if yes, place your trust in them and ask for advice but it is not necessary you follow that.. make it your own way... means to analyze it... think about every single consequence, positives, negatives, and every perspective of your decision then pick something which you think correct or best suits you.

- Read your page carefully don't let your mind and emotions over-empowered.. try to keep balance on them, it's time to close your eyes and just ask yourself none can give the best advice but it is.

- Just make your decision optimistically and with a blessed and grateful heart. It will do wonders, be hopeful, imaginative, energetic, and passionate towards your target.

THIS process can be followed when you have time to make a decision... but what to do when you have to make it instantly... for this type of situation you need to share your problem with your best one who had gone through that situation or you think can suggest you the best. Your life is the best teacher for YOU.... It first gives you a test then teaches you the lesson but always gives you a glimpse of the test so that you can grow for that... Use your experiences of life and the best thing will learn from others' mistakes and from your elder ones.

Have a wonderful moment!!!

FOUR

HAVING A AIM IS NECESSARY

The most irritating thing in our life is not having an idea of what is our aim... What leads our life to the future.. What skills we have.. If we know... then how should it be made our career? There are a lot of questions regarding these thoughts but the answers will be found in silence.

Ask these questions to you when you're in peace and alone because every important thought process needs brainstorming and it can be done when the environment you are living in, is peaceful and calm with positive energy. Your aim and willpower towards it should be that much power as you can't be dragged by your negativity if any arises. You can take help your elder ones and the person you believe in, as they suggest you all the best and worst thing about you and about your greatest strength. SO move on with the "POSITIVE, HOPEFUL AND CONFIDENT MIND".

FIVE

KEEP GOING ON

Some persons are irreplaceable as well as their importance in our life... But some of them meant to be leave or distanced that's where we learn life does not stop for anyone... It goes on and we have to move on just to catch up with the life... And always remember life has some important and unexpected gift for you in your journey... If you stop then life will also hold all them so the better thing will be... "KEEP GOING ON"

SIX

MENSTRUATION

Menstruations, a not so discussed topic in our society, a life-giving biological process in women's bodies. Why does it become a taboo among the people..?? So much ill traditions to follow during that period in some families, even have to live alone in a room without interacting with your family members.

Now as the people come ahead to talk about it, awareness increases but not at a satisfactory level, awareness still needs to be reached to the last mile people. There are many initiatives by the government to make sure every girl, who is in puberty level, get the sanitary pads, available in primary healthcare free of cost, even in government schools girls should be given those sanitary pads every month.

But the problem of degradation has started due to huge waste of sanitary napkins, disposed of in an inappropriate way (often, even biodegradable also not degraded), become a problem like disposal of plastics.

There are many options available to girls for hygienic periods like tampons and menstrual cups. The menstrual cup, a funnel shape cup, should be inserted into the vagina and the collected blood can be easily disposed of in soil, work as fertilizer. It is reusable for many years, comfortable, hygienic, cost-effective, can be used for 10 hours easily, available in every size, and environment friendly. Virginity loss fear also comes in many virgin women's minds so married women can easily prefer these cups.

SEVEN

Quotes By Pooja Singh

"Every achievement can't be said success... But every achievement is a step towards your success...."

ℙℙℙ

"Your present is just a outcome of your decisions and choices, you have made in your past....."

ℙℙℙ

"Labeling yourself that you are this type.. you are that type.. and always try to adjust yourself in a frame.. just come out from this comfort zone... there are a lot of things to explore in this world.. to add

up.. and also for the subtraction.. be like water.. can acquire any shape without loosing it's basic character.

ҏҏҏ

"

Keep no label for yourself.. recreate them

ҏҏҏ

"*Craving which harm your interest.... should be superseded by your Willpower.*"

ҏҏҏ

"*Sporadic parts of your self-confidence need to be collected failures can torn you but always give you a chance to reshape yourself, the way you want... move ahead and catch up with the speed of flow.*"

ҏҏҏ

"*Forward steps should be taken after releasing all your loads to the current situation and try to simplify them.. because with the increasing steps your loads will only enhance... instead of being a free person , you become a ass... loaded with the heavy weight of your own tensions , stress and problems. Your failures simply give you clues that your thought process and actions haven't yet match with the level of success."*

ᑭᑭᑭ

"Giving a good thought and it's imagination of fulfillment in breakfast to your mind is sufficient to maintain the stability of your mind for a good omen and awesome day."

ᑭᑭᑭ

"keep tracking your good thoughts. ..."

ᑭᑭᑭ

"Before going to sleep just recall all the events of the day even worse one and create imagination the way you want to let them happen for a best day ahead.."

ᑭᑭᑭ

"

.. ready to take flights but not to sit silently without giving a best trial.. it may be the 100th one."

ÞÞÞ

"*Sometimes only we can rejuvenate our energy by self praise.*"

ÞÞÞ

"*Loving yourself unconditionally... never let you feel down even when everything is happening odd, a confident smile still can be seen in your face.*"

ÞÞÞ

"*As the darkness is nothing but absence of light, problem is nothing but absence of an idea to find solution.. same as the gaps created by failures... filled by experiences and work like stairs(when you ruthlessly honest to yourself and just ask one question to your inner soul, "have you done your fullest...?? have you prepared yourself to be eligible for your desire.???" to get your desire of success.*"

ÞÞÞ

"Khud pr bharosa n Karne ki galti bahut bhari padti h.."

ᑭᑭᑭ

"

"Me :- Bhaiya....?? Bhaiya Haa.. beta" Just love this line"

ᑭᑭᑭ

"

Take your decision and prove them right because it's only you who can do it."

ᑭᑭᑭ

"Anything, over, leads you towards destruction.. even the positivity. So some amount of negativity is necessary because it will show you that you are not perfect , still a lot remaining to craft yourself and save you from becoming overconfident."

♡♡♡

"My life is my Kingdom.. only I decide what should be done with it."

♡♡♡

""INTROVERT", the most misunderstood person sometimes even by the closest one."

♡♡♡

"Best thing you can do.. just come out from your comfort zone."

♡♡♡

"Never ever let any person become your habit."

♡♡♡

"Passion followed by Profession leads you to the levels of achievements but profession followed by

passion leads you towards commercialisation your talent and degradation of quality of work."

ᐈᐈᐈ

"Never wait for the right time... When you start acting that will be right time."

ᐈᐈᐈ

"Nature has its own way of balancing itself so as yours.. balancing strategy varies with the individuals and define your level of personality, thought process and maturity."

ᐈᐈᐈ

"Why are the religious places so peaceful and have positive vibes.. ?? Almost all the people used to tell the God what they want, what should be end of their problems if they are facing some, what are their wishes which shows the positive nature of communication ; used to come with happy mind and for blessings if something good happen in their life and chanting of powerful verses , creat a positive surrounding around the premises and fill them with positive vibes and a sense of peace."

ღღღ

"Mind your words.. intentionally or unintentionally you are hurting someone by those set of words."

ღღღ

"In the aspire of making our life according to our wishes... We used to forget to make time to live our life."

ღღღ

"It is the matter of time... Plzzz.. wait I am about to reach my timezone..."

ღღღ

"It is the "time".... always changes it's companionship.. be aware..."

ღღღ

"Insano ki bhi numaishen lagti h .. or punchha jata h kon sa pasand h..."

ÞÞÞ

"Craving which harm your interest.... should be superseded by your Willpower."

ÞÞÞ

"Continuously thinking about our problems make us paralyze not physically but mentally... We become totally blank ..... Even, not able to think any more about other things.. everything seems like against u... whether it is in ur favour..."

ÞÞÞ

"Angels are working in the earth.... support and respect the front line worriers against "

ÞÞÞ

"Nature is playing her cards... Just to rebalance herself.."

ᑭᑭᑭ

"Kuchh logo se nafrat bhi isliye Hoti h... kyonki wo nafrat Karne ki koi wajah nhi dete..."

ᑭᑭᑭ

"Punchhne pr sab kuchh to theek hota h... Baat bas samjhane ki hoti h.. ki haa.. kuchh theek nhi h.."

ᑭᑭᑭ

"It's time to remove dust from fake yourself.. to know the real you."

ᑭᑭᑭ

"Just passionate about your dream.. if you let it go.... Someone else will make it happen owns... and you will only left with regret of not pursuing it."

ᑭᑭᑭ

"If you always choose to play in safe side. you will never be able to explore yourself because you have never taken risk.."

ღღღ

"Lamhe to yo hi guzarte jayenge pr.... Yade hamesha in lamhon ko sanjokar rakhegi.."

ღღღ

"Being an adult you have to pretend of being stronger enough to not let tears roll out.. life goes on with your people... without your people. your tears"

ღღღ

"Every Decision leads you somewhere it may be drag you in the worst situation, a dark sight, but teaches you one of the best lesson of life, steps you take to overcome from that situation make you a grown up person enough to not repeat that thought process again."

ღღღ

"Fulfillment of one wish become the reason of making more wishes.... Life after analysing the situations and time, queues up them, arrange some tests for every stage and said, "Clear them and move ahead step wise.""

ღღღ

"Old people become so stubborn that you can't resist yourself to get irritated while knowing that they are the guest of some days... enough to make you feel guilty."

ღღღ

"Your future is in your hand... Creat it or destroy it.. is also your choice.."

ღღღ

"Fake news and rumours used to work like the act of mindwash where you can't use your conscience.... and spread very rapidly to contain. So it's upto you

that if you get something like this and know that the information is wrong stop forwarding it and report it."

ϸϸϸ

"In these days... Barbie dolls sellers are struggling to make them look like as much natural as humans and humans are struggling to get the look like Barbie dolls... Isn't it something contradictory... Why can't we praise natural beauty which comes from inside...???"

ϸϸϸ

"Things, which used to be seemed like impossible or difficult in the past... now become the new normals or part of daily routine."

ϸϸϸ

"Apno se hare to kya hare.. wahan to haar kr bhi jeet k sukoon h..."

ϸϸϸ

"When the graph of our heart beats is not simple line because when it is, you are dead... So it's need to frequently up down, that's what happen in our life.. ups and downs in our life needed to realize our real potential and the life in real sense that it is all about surviving every second."

♡♡♡

"Something, someone, somewhere and somemoments are waiting for you ready to embrace them for sometimes."

♡♡♡

"Your all physical gestures are minutely monitored by your mind so give it the signal you want to feel... Even when you don't want to be happy because of anything you are going through.. still keep a smile on your face... It will make a big change in your life. TRY IT... IT REALLY WORKS.."

♡♡♡

"Not everything happening in life, is wished but needed to make the life move on for something

unknown and adventure."

ᢀᢀᢀ

"*Father is the first love of every girl and a hero & ideal for a boy... and a back bone for a family which is given shape by his wife. α Father is the first love of every girl and a hero & ideal for a boy... and a back bone for a family which is given shape by his wife.*"

ᢀᢀᢀ

"*When you're fed up with the events and failures after trying your best for that single thing... Just think of starting work on your second thought.*"

ᢀᢀᢀ

"*Yes!!!!... I am lucky... Every morning after getting up first thought should be," Thank you God for giving me this day of life" gives you a positive start and strength to do something productive.*"

ᢀᢀᢀ

"I am here and I will be here or not but my memories will always be here."

ᑭᑭᑭ

"I know everything will be all right... But when...?"

ᑭᑭᑭ

"Celebrate the self created beauty of your own and embrace your flaws just to restructure them for your better self creation."

ᑭᑭᑭ

"If a father is the back bone of a family... a mother gives the shape to that back bone. For a mother her child is always right but she knows how to make realize him/ her, his/her mistakes.. When she starts, everyone remembers pending work. Specially father and in case of children they start folding their clothes scattered here & there"

ᑭᑭᑭ

"Start your morning with this strong thought." I am the luckiest person of the day" to get a better day."

ᑭᑭᑭ

"Don't know from where to start... But surely know what to start.."

ᑭᑭᑭ

"Keep a smile on your face.. It is 90% enough to make jealous to your haters."

ᑭᑭᑭ

"Restrict yourself to tell your aspirations... Most of the people don't want that you move ahead in your life..."

ᑭᑭᑭ

"We need to accept our mistakes just to grow as a person and life lessons."

ᑭᑭᑭ

"In this earth everything has been given space to develop themselves and live peacefully.. if the place is encroached then conflict is inevitable."

ᑭᑭᑭ

"You want everything best for yourself but how will you get... if you don't work hard by giving your best.. THINK ABOUT IT!!!"

ᑭᑭᑭ

"Spread your arms...then hug yourself.. first step to start loving yourself.."

ᑭᑭᑭ

"Jindagi itni aasani se samajh aane wali cheej hi Hoti to abhi tk jindgi k liye ek rulebook ban gayi Hoti jise padkar sab jindagi k Sare rules Yaad kr Lete but aisa nhi h.... Life is different for everyone but it's destination is same.... The thing where your life can be differentiated from others... is the process of living"

ᐅᐅᐅ

"I'm the first and long lasting love of myself."

ᐅᐅᐅ

"When you can't keep yourself happy... You are just living your life not enjoying it."

ᐅᐅᐅ

"I don't know what are the things I want to do in my life as the wishes are unlimited... But I surely know what I don't want to do in my life..."

ᐅᐅᐅ

"

As we all have unlimited wishes and process of making wishes is like a nuclear reaction... One becomes the reason of making other wishes..... So having desires is natural but we all need to set boundaries and limitations so that our life goes on as per our standards..."

EIGHT

When you are in Approach – Avoidance

When you are in Approach - Avoidance conflict... just take a calculated risk... While knowing what can be the best as well as the worst outcome of your decision then prove it right... After all...!! the streets of the world are so busy.. where you have to create space for your steps as well as have to pave your own path to move ahead.. if you want to survive.. want to be satisfied... otherwise you will be crushed and the story of your dreams.. your desires.. will be end.

NINE

CONSTERNATION...

We all are striving to achieve our desires... A DESIRED LIFE...

At some point of time we have a sense of CONSTERNATION due to overthinking about things which totally ruin our mental stability and peace...

Don't worry these are the things which give us a sense of ALIVENESS. Whenever you think like" No ,I can't do it... It is totally IMPOSSIBLE". Make yourself realize that there is no existence of this word because the word itself says "IM POSSIBLE

So cheer up...!!!! you have nothing to cheat yourself and now only thing you know.. "YES IT IS POSSIBLE.... I CAN DO ANYTHING WHAT I WANT".

TEN

MAKE YOUR WISHES..

Fulfillment of one wish becomes the reason of making more wishes because it brings with it the sense of good omen and hope to your heart. Life always arrange some tests to check your eligibility for your wishes and prepares you for everything you want or anything going to make you mentally and emotionally stable & future ready. It includes everything, every person who is in your life or was in life or about to come... Your learning process ends with your death and every moment surprises you and gives a key to unlock your some hidden potential. Be warm with yourself and always try to be happy.... Hope for the best.

ELEVEN

LOVE AND HATE

As both are contradictory to each other... But if one talk about hate, these are the things... one's mind is not ready to accept them. When we talk about people whom we hate.. actually we don't hate people but their habits. But the people we love, we usually avoid these habits... Because we don't want to lose them. But at certain point of time we can't avoid these habits and start hating the most loved people.

Sometimes when we can't express our love... that love change into anger and anger simply change into hate. This also happen in our life.

So the solution is whatever you feel for someone just express your feelings... no matter for whom, it may be your parents, friends or anyone else.. but keep in mind the relationship you have with that person while telling them... I usually hug my mom because this hug shows my love towards my mom without saying a word...

TWELVE

LET ME LINE

THIS ALL HAPPENED IN ONE NIGHT..... a Thinking about how to approach my lifel my aim).. Suddenly a thought of failure came to my mind.... totally destroyed my self confidence which have been built after a lot of effort by my self intuition......I was just about to cry, my eyes filed with tears.. Somewhere a continuous failure breaks you and your self confidence too.... The stage where you don't even try to stand up again.. and start your journey.. But the dream which has been nourished in my mind don't want to die.. it force me every minute to take further steps and said..," Let me live.!!!!"

THIRTEEN

LET YOUR FEELINGS OUT

Relationship is all about proportionality... If you don't let your feelings out, you can lose the closest one from your life... People who loves you understand you but sometimes they want to listen and feel what you feel about them.. so let it be expressed... In your way... start from the minimum but do start expressing your feelings to your loved ones. You don't need to do it in high or critical way, people who closed to you feel above the sky if you do it in simple way... So do it.

9 798885 309325

Printed by Libri Plureos GmbH in Hamburg, Germany